NOSTALGIA for
the CRIMINAL PAST

NOSTALGIA for the CRIMINAL PAST

poems

Kathleen Winter

For Cintia,
with pleasure of seeing you again
at the Napa Valley Writers Conference.
Best wishes for your poetry —
Kathleen
July 30, 2013

Elixir Press
Denver, Colorado

www.elixirpress.com

Many thanks to the editors of these publications, in which the following poems originally appeared, sometimes in slightly different versions:

32 Poems: "Gulf of Mexico"; AGNI: "Hamster Thrown From Monster Truck"; Anti-: "Homage to Homage"; Barrow Street: "Country Club Fourth of July"; Cerise Press: "Bathing at the Museum," "Third Eye," "Wrong Sonnet: Mystery"; Ekphrasis: "The McNay"; FIELD: "Morning Poem"; Legal Studies Forum: "Morning"; Memorious: "Nostalgia for the Criminal Past"; Parthenon West Review: "Animal Philosophy," "Rabbit," "Snapshot of a Boxer"; Slope: "Perfect Loser," "Petit Magritte," "Post Hoc Ergo Propter Hoc"; So to Speak: "Overheard antique men"; Studio: "Dreamy"; The Cincinnati Review: "Nostalgia for Apollo," "The Beat," "The Rain," "West Lake Hills"; The New Republic: "Eschatology," "Wrong Sonnet: Multiplicity"; The Southeast Review: "Jellyfish Elvis"; VOLT: "I sleep with Patriarchy."

"Incarnation," "Mitosis," "Morning," "December Pastoral," "Overheard antique men," "Perfect Loser," "Petit Magritte" "Post Hoc Ergo Propter Hoc" and "The McNay" appeared in Invisible Pictures, a chapbook published by Finishing Line Press.

Cover art: Russell Lee, June 1939; Library of Congress, Prints & Photographs Division, FSA/OWI Collection, LC-USF34-0333417-D, *Migrant worker looking through back window of automobile near Prague, Oklahoma.* Lincoln County, Oklahoma.

Book design by Steven Seighman

Library of Congress Cataloging-in-Publication Data

Winter, Kathleen, 1961-
Nostalgia for the criminal past : poems / Kathleen Winter.
    p. cm.
Includes bibliographical references and index.
ISBN 978-1-932418-44-6 (alk. paper)
I. Title.
PS3623.I6724N67 2012
811'.6—dc23

2011046265

First Elixir Press edition: 2012

10   9   8   7   6   5   4   3   2   1

For Greg

CONTENTS

ACKNOWLEDGMENTS

Love and gratitude to my teachers at ASU, my family, and friends, many of whom read and responded to this manuscript while it was in process. I thank Vermont Studio Center and the artists met there, and everyone connected with the Prague Summer Program.

Special thanks to Tim Gray, Allison Moseley, Francie Salle, Julia Lingys and John Carlisle, Sophia Park, Paul Ocampo, Rick Eddy, Finnegan Winter-Campbell, and the Cummins family, for their inspiration and encouragement.

Warm thanks to Dana Curtis, Elixir Press, and Deborah Bogen.

For the life and memory of Charles D. Winter, Jr.

NOSTALGIA for
the CRIMINAL PAST

INTRODUCTION

Kathleen Winter opens *Nostalgia for the Criminal Past* with an epigraph from Virginia Woolf, "I do not believe in separation. We are not single…" yet this impressively mature and intelligent debut collection challenges that sentiment, sifting through experience to establish a separation that allows both a sense of the singular self and a more conscious relatedness. In Winter's poetry this is not limited to the more usual marking of a distinction between self and parent or self and lover. She's ambitious and her obsessions include examining the self exactly as it presents itself, end-stopped by animal mortality, but alive for a time in a great geological theater, constantly related to other natural creatures as well the rocks and the seas, and to a creation "troubled in a way /that means no harm to anyone." ("Snapshot of a Boxer")

Winter is interested in how those relationships work and the book opens with poems that explore a few possibilities. There are relationships based on a childish, naïve and self-involved simplicity expressed in the title poem:

> Those days, we never saved. We never went to a bank
> except to rob it. The getaway car had no parts to
> control smoke, our escape route lost in a plume of
> poisons….
> "Nostalgia for the Criminal Past"

Then there's the perhaps similarly childish but more polite and disciplined belief of many of us raised in the fifties and sixties:

> Back then, back there, the handsome astronauts
> could build their own machines,
>
> …I miss their elevated heart-rates
> At the take-off, god-like, their views of Earth's

swirled atmosphere,
...their quaint
faith in our nation, their quaint male
universe in which I was a lovely
and a silent child.

                    "Nostalgia for Apollo"

But these depictions of childhood's mental states are merely a jumping
off place for Winter. She's gifted with an imagination that considers most
things from new and irreverent angles. In "Escape from Eden," for exam-
ple, she complains, on Eve's behalf, that Biblical paradise must have been
essentially boring: "there was nothing *at / stake*. We didn't feel pain...
We couldn't even bicker / to pass the time." In this provocative poem,
Eve's artistic streak rescues her from a tedious eternal passivity. She no-
tices that when a snake swallows a pig "That pig made a change in the
snake's flat line." Reversing the Biblical myth of the snake whispering to
Eve, Winter depicts the first woman as the instigator of action. Looking
at Adam she imagines how she and that snake might put something at
stake, how she might get God's attention.

Animals and art appear regularly in Winter's work. Interestingly, she
doesn't oppose "human" and "animal", but sees our human mental and
emotional identity as one part of our animal existence. For this poet, art
seems to be the ultimately human activity, but she is clear that in no way
does it save us from our animal fate.

I keep going
back to dead animals.
Like live ones, they take us.
Lorca, *por ejemplo*,
borne by dead animals
to solemn gardens
tacky with blood, Neruda

by dead animals carried

again to the sea,
Desnos riding a dead mule
through the Marais…
                    "December Pastoral"

And

The fish leap laterally
Out of the sea, silver,
Slightly at a slant, and plop
Back in, graceless,
Against our expectation.
I am such an animal.
                    "Mustang Island Suite"

So Winter is moved to examine the looming presence of death, and how that affects the ability to be a self, related to others and the greater world. In what is certainly one of the more articulate expressions of that painful puzzle she writes "Grey pelt of mouse limp in injury/ beneath the kitchen's leaking ceiling…// The bait was irony working again,//the irony of nothing, taking/ so much of our attention,// ripping us again and again/ out of our upholstered moment." ("Eschatology")

Section II of *Nostalgia* gives us poems in which Winter faces that issue in a personal arena. "Mustang Island Suite" takes place on a visit to her aging parents, and here we get a sure feel for the body as a separate agent, unaffected by our will:

Surely we come to this state
In astonishment
That the bodies we know best
Could elude us in unexpected abdications,
A failure of the cells we can see
And of those on the inside
That negotiate coldly with our doctors

But Winter is not just concerned with deaths that are personal to us. She forthrightly considers the deaths we cause, not only the mouse on the trap, but the accidental moments when attention slips and we become fatally dangerous ourselves.

>...On the winding road I tried to remember how
>easy it would be to kill someone accidentally and how the time I did I
>hadn't been in the car at all...
>>"Morning Poem"

All this tough reality is offset in Section III where Winter gives us a frenzied account of amorous recklessness in which desperation pushes the speaker from one risky venture to another. She visits the State Fair with the devil, is beat up on the street, but determines "If the gangling shadow of desire / is shame, then let me face them: golden husk / of the owl-rung instant before dusk." ("Eve Smoking")

These poems reflect the feverish hysterical attitudes most often associated with adolescence. But eventually Eve returns, somehow tied to the very paradise she worked earlier to destroy, forcing the poet to consider happiness, or if not happiness, at least love. In the book's final section, the self is once again an actor and it wants what a self wants - the other. It wants love and sex and music and it can have those things, Winter tells us, but temporarily. Here the poet is united and re-united with the lover, with avocados and apples, and with the pleasure of being a voice. In "Third Eye" she writes:

>You tell me, Science,
>the mouse in my stomach is doubt
>>is the animal fear   wriggling

>yet   sleeping naked I go closer to beloved
>you naked in a distant state

There is a maturity here that we aim for, a looking into the dark and an eschewing of despair as she writes "part of the eye has seen loss/ part waits for it—". Still, she is able to write "a grey horse settles down on kitchen floor/ before we touch her—/ gladness fills the room// sunning the waiting…" This, then, is the synthesis of art and animality, an emotional intelligent opening that leans toward its possibilities even as it honors its limitations.

I once heard a lecture in which Ellen Bryant Voigt said that whenever the poet writes, she's the bird on the branch singing "my song, my song, my song." *Nostalgia for the Criminal Past* is Kathleen Winter's complicated, insightful, intriguing, sometimes sad and always artful song. It is my privilege to introduce her to you.

Deborah Bogen
Judge, Elixir Press Poetry Awards

I

One sees a fin passing far out.

* * *

I do not believe in separation. We are not single.

—*Virginia Woolf*

Nostalgia for the Criminal Past

Those days, we never saved. We never went to a bank except to rob it. The getaway car had no parts to control smoke, our escape route lost in a plume of poisons. We hid on a hill where nobody went; it shot straight up. Even animals were winded when they got to the top—raccoons, red foxes passing out on the gingerbread porch. We let our hair grow wild, we never paid taxes. There's nothing that wouldn't grow there, soil seething with worms, fog slithering over the oaks, sun going and coming erratically—an occasional god. It was warm sometimes, dogs snoring on the beds, on the green couch stuffed with surfaces of birds. Like the children, we were naked: it gave us time to read. Not having to dress, to do laundry, we built silos of time in which to drown.

Snapshot of a Boxer

You sat with your back to the baby,
guarding him against the color green,
the insistence of steeples.
The eight a.m. sun moved out from clouds
like a well-trained MBA
adjusting to changed conditions.
A fleck from Earth's veneer of life,
you had your memories,
your sensitivities to sounds, to smells,
to expressions like the British *barking mad*.
No one had to tell you
cleverness is not a virtue.
In the quick distance,
playground's empty geometry
stood by to be embodied.
You waited soundlessly, knowing
the creation is troubled in a way
that means no harm to anyone.
You waited for one of those people
who think they own trees,
own animals, to look in your direction.

Nostalgia for Apollo

Back then, back there, the handsome astronauts
could build their own machines,
each man assigned a wing, a plan, a system to design.
In their white shirts, in their thin ties, they worked it out.
At cocktail parties, on cocktail napkins
at the bar, they synchronized the rendezvous
of master ship with its squat module, or, alone
in their well-ordered minds, they engineered
the right thing for a man to say when stepping off
the last rung onto lunar dust, just after taking
a piss on the ladder. I miss their gravity-free
cantering across the fields of the moon,
their silent, patient waving from behind curved
glass, their close-cropped hair, their Mission Control cigars,
their guts. I miss their elevated heart-rates
at the takeoff, god-like, their views of Earth's
swirled atmosphere, their cowboy tendency
to terseness, their ticker-tape parades, their quaint
faith in our nation, their quaint male
universe in which I was a lovely
and a silent child.

Animal Philosophy

we nod, peck & gesture our spoonfuls
to a little night music, crunch
of the obvious being consumed
by mystery, now the horrifying
death cry of the obvious
being dismembered among firs

there's room for three in this bed
so why is our idea of the possible
so slim, always the same haircut?
even an object
lifeless as antique mannequin's
grey canvas gives pleasure of texture
O circler
O fragile ice-skater

so settle, let your fur glisten against me
& still you growl as though this chill
were meant for you, American dog,
post-Enlightenment individualist
licking, licking away at your
self, persisting

Homage to Homage

Penumbra's a conundrum,
conundrum is penumbra.
An umbrella's humdrum—

an elision. Humdrum
as a striking out, elision.
There is no dearth

of little forks.
To fashion a remedy,
a remedy of friction,

Townsend's big-eared bat
and pallid bat and pallid bat—
an ashen bat.

A mighty swat, a balk.
A leaking out about a tank.
O big-eared bat,

a drumming strike,
a remedy of little dearth.
There is no humdrum

remedy, pallid as and is.
Penumbra is a leaking out,
a lightwave, umbrella-ed about.

Of homage to elision,
there's no dearth.
Conundrum is a little balk.

Jellyfish Elvis

When my aunt by marriage Aunt Noreen
was in the beach movie with Elvis and she said his toenails were too long
I used to think it all was her, he couldn't be the slob she took him for,
that all that crap about his breath being a bomb,
his table manners like an Army mess,
his undershirts rust-stained and even his eyebrows permanently out of whack
was just a bunch of sour grapes that she cooked up
to balance for the fact that she was cut out of the picture after it had wrapped,
in spite of how it hardly was *her* fault about the man-o-war
that stung her shin during the kissing scene with Elvis and a couple other girls
when he was grabbing her around her waist
and had his tongue she swears half down her throat
when like a fireball or a billion ant bites all at once
the tentacle associated with her leg.
And naturally without a chance to think about it—even to cry out—
she bit him, hard.
But other stuff's come out about him, pills and funny sandwiches,
and dry old bird she is, Noreen still has the scar.

Escape From Eden

Every dawn was the same: waking to a symphony of waterfalls, the larks, tree-frogs trilling in the forest. Then nothing to do except play among flowers and vines, tease the beasts and eat and sleep. God was absent, or at least invisible, silent. Time after time I'd call to him but the only reply was a cold afternoon shower and that may have been coincidence, his way of cleaning dust off the leaves and the petals.

All Adam wanted to do was sleep. He was expert at it. He was so still, stretched out naked on ferns, I don't think he ever dreamed. His chest rose with mind-numbing regularity.

Our food was vegetarian, wheat and greens for millennia, no steak. In fact there was nothing *at stake*. We didn't feel pain, so if there was pleasure how were we to know it? We couldn't even bicker to pass the time.

Finally I started to study the animals: the best spectacle for centuries was the boa constrictor, patiently swallowing the pig beneath an apple tree. That pig made a change in the snake's flat line. It gave me an idea.

When Adam was asleep and the snake was hungry again, I whispered that the man might make a fortifying meal. I figured if anything could get God's attention it was something happening to Adam.

Hamster Thrown From Monster Truck

This is the headline from *The Onion*
we love best.

                    What does this say
     about us?

At least our schadenfreude's minimalist?

Neither of us ever had a hamster
for a pet.

     Or even knew one as a friend's
     pet

          or the teacher's pet: a hamster for the masses
          of a third grade class, for instance;

nor do we know anything of gerbils.

          Not on their own account,
               neither their relationship to hamsters.

But monster trucks—
these we've seen.

               Monsters of all models, guzzlers

          on the byways of our humble town,

rumbling above us at the stoplight
like a frisky two-story building,

                              charging forward at the change
              on super-sized tires,

swinging, sometimes, from the bumper

a pair of balls.

The hamster's monster truck has thrown him
for a loop.

              We think it probably shook him up.

He took the last lap of the treadmill-track too fast!

        Fans in the bleachers standing
on their seats,

              the sun a beer-haze through their shades.

We hope the hamster's landed
on his feet.

Petit Magritte

A miniature is a gift.
A minotaur is a bull?

A wooden horse is no gift
and a bum steer is no bull.

My lover, a matador,
a matador my lover.

Give me over, racedriver.
A jacket with handwarmer

pockets, a rabbit collar.
Here in the City of Light

nobody has a dollar.

Overheard antique men

hanker for things ancient as bad manners,
consider "what all women do" in front of you

like you're furniture,
like you, like her, "just wanna get hooked up"

into what? you wonder, peering further
into Sold hope chest, spotted mirror—

some outmoded contraption:
he, proud Morgan, you, the plough.

December Pastoral

The dull red hole
was the vultures' bowl,
the hide, their tablecloth.
These birds made the deer
so dead it became the earth,
the winter earth, the earth's white fur.

I keep going
back to dead animals.
Like live ones, they take us.
Lorca, *por ejemplo*,
borne by dead animals
to solemn gardens
tacky with blood, Neruda

by dead animals carried
again to the sea,
Desnos riding a dead mule
through the Marais, intestinal,
toward his cabaret. We, too,
taken by the rotten
to a highway years,

miles, from this page,
past necessity's banquet:
the guests' unruffled serenity
in black, all their ankles
slender over the host as,
clean of remorse,
they gouge and gorge.

Country Club Fourth of July

Mother is out of breath with it—
the studded gladiator sandal—

the newsprint ad for it
which thrills her cloistered heart

and strains the worked-up muscles
of her chest.

American crawl, propel me,
small and hungry, gripping

a plastic bag,
toward the bounty of illusion

water magnifies:
thousands of goldfish and coins

tossed in the luminous
chemical pool.

Morning

they come as promised
and fractional gifts

our dreams of the dead

we live with them
to lose them over again

to hunt them in the skittering
instant of waking

as owl scours darkness
for quick tendernesses

our parents' careless faces
explain themselves in terms

we understand
invented by our longing

Perfect Loser

I want always
to lose right,
to toss everything

necessary, nothing
overly, to know
cold what

other's worth
retaining:
me, the mollusk,

lapping sap,
making it, slow,
blind, into myself.

Eschatology

In the long run, we are all dead.
—John Maynard Keynes

Grey pelt of mouse limp in injury
beneath the kitchen's leaking ceiling,

grey subtraction. I crouch in a cramped
room displacing my mind, trying to put it

for an instant into your body.
The bait was irony working again,

you can taste the bitter end.
Perhaps you somehow know

there's nothing to be afraid of:
the irony of nothing, taking

so much of our attention,
power of the vacuum

ripping us again and again
out of our upholstered moment.

II

Morning Poem

Yesterday I asked myself again if life can be corrupted by what you don't remember. Greg was on the phone waiting for my steel cut oats to simmer for the minimum half hour, to collapse and dissolve. When he told someone *she likes the oil paint version of oatmeal and I like the acrylic* I thought it might fit into a morning poem that spoke about the Steins' long-haired trophy cows, how the puny straw-colored cow had looked like she'd just woken up, the forelock veiling her amber eyes and clumps of coarse hair stiffening all over her torso into peaks pointing different directions, whipped-hard egg whites, and me sliding past the field on the way to class comparing the car clock to the clock on the tape deck to the wristwatch, each set ahead of reality in varying degrees. On the winding road I tried to remember how easy it would be to kill someone accidentally and how the time I did I hadn't been in the car at all and it had been empty, slowly rolling heavily backward and she much older and perhaps not hearing it at first, walking away outside as I was reaching for ice cream, for a loaf of bread. How she hadn't looked dead but only pale and almost naked as they tried to save her with their bare hands, then with a kit of blade and sparks, while I watched from a few yards apart as she lay still and more still and more still.

Postcard 1923: Detail of a Laundress

Grace Finney can't live through the night.
        As ever, Mother, she imagines herself
    free—dropping heavy as her black iron
                through sheets of altostratus,
        through linen shirts and lace blouses,
smashing like a barrel
                through Niagara's filigree
        where Annie Edson Taylor said she'd
never do *that* again, plunging
    from Earth faster than blind Sonora Carver
                diving a roan
        from the top of the sixty-foot tower
into a metal pool.
                The weight of faith hastens her
        from bluestarch, backache,
burns and cabbage, from radishes
                    and fennel grown wild
        by the roadside,
    away from cider and weak tea.
Aggressive descender,
            she swoops through the hours:

                the ballast of a tumor
                hurries her toward God.

The McNay

after Kay Sage's self-portrait, *Le Passage*

The trouble is, I always want to go there
with you. When we exit the museum into the devil heat
I place my hand in yours, your sockless loafered steps
are slow. You know your shins are sticks,
your mouth is dry, your elegant, strong feet
and hands now oversized like the Burghers' bronze ones.

We angle into shade to talk about the work:
Sage's canvas with her back turned toward us
as she faces a featureless plain,
paint's language singing her dirge
for Tanguy, her vision landscape nightmare
monotony upset by the beauty of the back
of her left arm, the beauty of her naked back,
her self understanding.

We know you're going;
how can anybody help it?
I know despair's pathology,
that the world could never be
so bland, so flat as that suicide
scenery, yet I still can't see
how it will ever be okay for me
for you to leave it.

Mustang Island Suite

I

Sand in my eye; cold in both directions.
How clean to go down when the tide is out
And see, and see, and see.
Loosen, obsolete idea of beauty,
Concede to Gulf's debris:
Three-foot red snapper body, carcasses
Of catfish slunk in the grey grains,
Fleet of whiskered submarines submerging;
Rays, white, rotting; cartilage, bits of joints
Plastic in an antique definition.
The jacket pocket makes a third hanging
Breast to fill with shells while shuffling
Windward on a run so desultory
I can pick out shrimp holes
And twisting, inch-long tornadoes,
Frozen, with a glaze: white on beige.
A girl sings
In a separate room. I covered myself
With layers as these creatures did
When nakedness did not serve me.
The speck will lodge all day
In invisible membrane beneath my
Sea-green eye, tune stuck in my head.

II

Did you meet her, the mother of the dogs?
My mother asks, and bares her prejudice
For the canine inhabitants of this
Most human-altered place, erstwhile marshes
Filled up by golf courses, subdivisions
Of beach houses pastel under fog-drift.
How absurd we are to collar them, so,
But talk to and of them like children free
To age out of their helplessness,
To move upland, inland, to habitate
Unsentimental space, childless and earth-toned.

III

The fish leap laterally
Out of the sea, silver,
Slightly at a slant, and plop
Back in, graceless,
Against our expectation.
I am such an animal.

Loose in the Gulf, beneath
These grey-green waves,
There is nothing to bind me
To the shoes, the clothes,
Phone and watch behind me,
Where pickup trucks and
Flagpoles stalk the sand.

IV

My father deserves to have a god.
It's years since he moved easily,
Without any pain.
Even if nature is all some of us have
To be afraid of, even if it's only our own,
Surely we come to this state
In astonishment
That the bodies we know best
Could elude us in unexpected abdications,
A failure of the cells we can see
And of those on the inside
That negotiate coldly with our doctors.

So here he is
In the Port Aransas swimming pool,
Gulls overhead under clouds
Greyed with rain, looking up
But unable to get out
Without the ladder.
To get to it he'll have to paddle
Slowly, upright through deep water,
His pale arms politely failing him,
The muscles gesturing
Goodbye before his will
Can will to going.

Cape Architecture

The bled white
                        morning light
            of being
in small towns
            with nothing to connect you
to them—
no dog in the alley
            no face or street corner,
drugstore   or barber.

Cold October light

pinioning facades
of antique
                New England.
Stopping time,
                        if it were not for the wind
coming out of the oil paint—
if it were not for a newspaper
                            striking the sidewalk,
        an ice cream vendor's
                        uneasy tinkling.
All we marry,
all we bear—
                    simply to avoid these frames.

Yuma Evening

Fire broke out
from a portion of the heart
as ocotillo springs
from the history of rock, angling
spines toward a colander of stars.

The flames took acres
of cotton bolls — of time —
of breath — altering them
from their element
as engines screamed
out of another county.

Sweat-rimed, smoking,
in the smell of the blaze
the men lean on their trucks,
doubting their lungs
could ever fail, doubting
the raptor heart could smolder,

combust and ascend.

Polis

From a distance she sees
as plumage the extravagant branches,
pine needles aligned toward

earth, through glass
and amplified breath
she sees festivities

of green blurred above
twin vertical limbs, a bantam
in britches, *consequence,*

the careless fingers
gesturing quotation as,
behind the speaker,

silent elongated drops stretch
from the edge of the tower's
roof to planted ground,

rainwater continuing
the atmosphere to root, beyond
root to limestone aquifer,

beyond aquifer to repose,
to calcification, and from that
halting to what end, this place?

West Lake Hills

As I love you from the distance of a marriage,
from the distance of infrequent visits,
your life appears to me like the far west ridge
silhouetted against pale sunset:
obscure in texture and detail, unapproachable
but bearing a definitive, calcitic edge.
In twenty years, everything you've said
about your childhood makes just
the jagged outline riding dark beneath,
where the rest of that story silently
petrifies, bones of the living beings
lost to you, lost inside you,
turning to mineral in the potent
chemical immersion, experience
unspoken.

Grey Muzzle

You signal from solitude, fretful
slotted days you try to translate
with mere words. San Francisco's
crusted barnacles gorgeously pale
across the Bay. This bus rattles to it.
Miles east, a filament of bridge
slings curves above the roadbed, spine.
Again I read myself vertiginous
when I should watch land move swiftly
backwards, more lush, more various
than language. Lean, contagious lover,
in that tunnel I found the clean
jewels of light. I left a sign for you
before I packed and disappeared—
hurled rock at a fir near the waterfall,
marked hard wet bark with a cluster
of red dust. Winter rained down
the tight channel, around boulders
grown in the stream, but the dog
could not hold still for us, or be black
as I'll search to remember.

Orienteering

for N.D.

Fever tries to sweat me out of bed. Good my astragalus,
commend me to your attentions. If my master could see
the monster my dreams made me into—
The minute I get to Paris, I said, *I want to buy shoes.*

God, the dear old words, your name in vain lingering
on my tongue or stuck half down the throat, a chicken bone,
size of a crutch. In this pique I'll talk with my teacher
through the ether, through a threadbare hood.

Streets midnighted by surviving trees, pecan, mock orange,
it neighbors indifferent atmosphere of the tinseled city north,
reclining at the river's hinge. Without children or religion,
where am I now but on a mattress, cold flat on the floor,
the bed I keep remaking.

Rabbit

A pet-store rabbit is loose
on Sonoma Mountain—

furtive but bright white, elliptical,
low to the ground, scuttering

(not exactly greased lightning
on those rabbit's-foot feet)

across the road at dawn.
Last week my husband spotted it

against the autumn weeds.
How that beast survives

one day to the next is mystery
to me, how it came to be

here
& what furred or feathery

inevitable will snatch it up, feel
the shudder of its misplaced life.

Terroir

I'm going backwards. Soon
I'll be in that bed again
gouged by the dog's-teeth Braille

that reads frustration,
layered on,
thick upon, itself.

Hundreds of pits pock the oak footboard.
To see it breeds
meaning, even before you run

your hand over it.
For three years I've been out of range,
but now I'm wheeling

past the military wastelands,
over the Mojave,
through Death Valley

to where ocean asserts heroics
against the hurting eye.
The eye that, in its rage, can see no damage.

Last night a long cacophony—
coyotes' frenzied screaming
ripped dry air above the park.

I stood still in time
to catch two, tearing upward on the cactus hill,
hellbent to join the fight.

I thought it was pain,
teething, that urged my dog
to attack the wood—

Or could he have been happy
as he sank his new teeth into it—
canines sharp white

in the blinding slit of time
when, primal, he rose over wooded
slopes faster than gravity.

Edge of February

Out past the animals, this afternoon's austere Pacific
has never needed us.

          Winter-thick heifers,
lambs with schoolgirl shins in black knee-socks,
what do they care if Egypt's freed of oligarchy?

Today, with plenty of sleep and strong coffee,
I'm making a miniature, flexible heaven
within my ribs.
              It includes each one of them.

But if some end up in my stomach later,
it won't surprise my friends.

My lover is elsewhere.

            Down the steep hill
in the ocean I find his grey-blue hair.

I see in him this Cooper's hawk
that has no patience with my scrutiny.

Between the truck and the bird's fencepost
winds a solid line—thin county road,
               impermeable
asphalt between fields
          the hawk appears to squint at,

looking past me to sheep and the ocean's organless
surface,

      stainless in the distance.

Joy is brief.

      It turns away, extends
its limbs,

      feathered, reptilian.

III

Dreamy

When I meet the Devil, handsome he and me
fly in a vivid little airplane at the State Fair,
dangling from a chain—

we're laughing, circling through the neon night,
our transportation tethered to a pole—

when the show tunes and the engine sounds
cut out, people I love perceive me
cryptically from the ground.

Cut Flowers

In the event of anything
I can, like the drying stems,
lie down, my color gold
of streetlights
vague in fog
above their military bearings.

The physicality of mental acts
courses carelessly through blind
blood alleys, a particle descends
through milky water
in a sphere of glass, we have
hit bottom.

He is gnawing at the leaves,
he has X's all over him,
is contagious.
When he is bent and active
there is nothing to do
but flatten ourselves

and smell earth—
a squalid vase,
a dime store cologne,
his teeth fretting our stems
with merciless dominion.

Kenmore Square

the sweltering
the shame (he puts away

his fist) of being
at the center

of their stares, the streetlights'
revelations

the beginning of the bruise—
when
winded

I linger
like a sandbag
on the sidewalk

at his feet

outside the pub's
front door, black
mouth

near Fenway Park
this rectangle of streets

brick buildings bearing
billboard promises

of sex
        of lightness

Mia Vita Violenta

Scratch that. Scratch into that
sound to mark where it stops,
where silence lies, bone hard

under tufts. Slip your hand
into it not knowing what you'll
get, get a handful of slender

cylindrical wet, what slips, what slops
between fingertips, mess of a joke,
that risk. How many red lights

have you crossed, how many acids
etched, how many roll-your-eyes
cross-your-fingers loves tossed?

A chip (a figure?) for each
spouse, chip for each loss,
chip for the clang in the guts

of the house, heating system's
rhythmical bent, urgency of it,
metallic, in your tin ear.

Does it make you shake to read
yellowed letters, the lunacy?
To see your dead pal drink beer

in her serial earrings inside your old
flat, picture parrot of grey-scale dots
on your hard husband's hat?

The thought you could've,
but never killed him—
like total environmental debacle,

it may be too distant to lament
but it's too possible, too actual,
to disbelieve.

I sleep with Patriarchy

in his tent that looks out over the world.
Light sheds white leaves
between leaves of the *sliva* trees.
To get the grass right
I'll need some black paint.
The present is an umbrella. Now
opens and closes each of its zillion eyes.
Patriarchy must mark everything
with intention. His tail
wakens at the base of my spine.

I believe it will be mine.

Eve Smoking

That garden we got ourselves towed out of—
did I even want to park there?
With this smoke
I think to replace hunger.
The grocer's beauty is an echo of yours, lover,

so I avoid the aisles of avocados,
apples, anything with seeds.
But what will break the fast,
and when appearing?
Lately, sublimation's lost its glamour—
the gesture's just a drag.

But *something* continues, combustion of body,
or merely leaves? Paper to ash, a grey drifting
scarf on breath, lust held in the mouth,
the exhalation without swallowing—
and yet, this mimic of abstention
sickens all the same.

      If the gangling shadow of desire
is shame, then let me face them: golden husk
of the owl-rung   instant before dusk.

IV

Wrong Sonnet: Multiplicity

My husband asks Why don't you write a poem
about why you like Virginia Woolf when
nobody else does.
The excruciating detail of a marriage
is what I like, I say, the drifting
in and out of Clarissa's mind and into Peter's,
how they notice the flow of London traffic
as a living animal, how they feel
themselves distributed in sub-atomic
bits into each other and over the city's squares
and towers, out into the hedgerows, the waves.
But Clarissa wasn't married to Peter
he would say, if he'd read it, she was
married to Richard. And I'd say
maybe she was, maybe she was.

Post Hoc Ergo Propter Hoc

This is the splendor
of calm love, the room
white on the inside
and on the outside.
Fed by the moon, dune
grass grows barnacles
of burr. Even innocence
has consequences.
So what if you talk
on the telephone
now and touch yourself
instead of taking
his fingers into
your mouth, almost
swallowing them—
at least you can sleep
with yourself afterward.

Gulf of Mexico

Flesh-colored mouth of the snake
blossoming in the border patrol's
limestone mind, confederates
in boredom.

The only glamorous thing
on the Pumpville road
is Crested Caracara, black
and white and crimson,
pairs of them stalled
in the attics of mesquites,
hungry for disaster.

We wheel through this thirst,
this boarded-up, broken down
wing of a state, toward the relief
of the Gulf: oaks bent inland
like arthritic digits, my grandmother's hands.

Flat water offers up, extends for miles
its tired salute, a lifetime of echoes rising,
coming on, the Christmas music.

***

Holding the overgrown
trade paperback against my knees
I circumnavigate
a symbol: Melville's *vivacious fish*,
capacity sufficient for a century
or three.

The dog's a stone-black flounder
on the sheets. His legs twitch
to the twang of the banjo.
To the longing
in my gut—my unfathomable—
I write back.

Ishmael asked *God keep me*
from ever completing anything.
The musician believes he has
forty years to make love to me—
why should he
hurry now.

Mitosis

Roads below are faint thread
tracery, spun by New Mexican
necessity: one-horse town to hitch
its ice-house to the truckstop.
Clouds distill shadow
over prairies,
momentary as a hare on the road
before the dogs see.
My love, an accident

attaches to the bones.
It permeates the layers of skin,
the mat of veins, it dawdles in nuclei
of cells that must divide to continue.
When we come together, I'm broken
as I hope I'll ever be.
Let us always share this
traveling toward again
dividing from each other.

The Bath

When I was a punk kid I'd
take a bath to hear myself think:
you are *you*, the *only* you, my
brain would say—
true or not—the crown of head just
over water, little island, dry brown
hair, my neck and shoulders bent
to the bathtub's ivory curve,
but both ears underwater
in that echo chamber
water made,
which amplified my thoughts till,
swelling, thought's voice filled the tub,
past the bathroom's framing,
busting limestone walls
& leaping boxwood hedges,
thinking being
—or becoming—everything.

The Beat

Busy busy busy, the Baroque.
Tonight, home at eleven,
have to shut it off.
A dozen feet away, he sleeps.
For him the music possibly goes on.
Avid notes that don't spare time for breath.
My mind paws at itself, its pest.
Hot spot, a supperclub of lust.
With this slow surge and thrust
Baroque would clash.
You need a languid rhythm that can last,
a rocking, swaying, bent-kneed push.
All day, my mind from side to side
swayed to the beat of lust.
I wanted it, and wanted it to stop.
All day, from side to side,
the beat of lust.
I wanted it, but wanted it to stop.
From side to side,
my mind swayed to the beat.
I wanted it and wanted it
to stop.

Bathing at the Museum

Casablanca lilies, sandbag mammaries—
what have you to do
with me?

Angels announce among flowers,
the monk's miniature carnations exquisitely
foregrounded.

There is no red
but the red of the deep
of the body.

Penitence is an unlikely fate
yet churches everywhere: incomprehensible
but for the rationality of tithes.

Like Bonnard's wife
incessantly I bathe, sensations of liquid
intervening between mind

& body, blurring animosities.
In dim flux the mind begins to lift,
words shimmer,

jewel-hued in their tissues.
Wreckage of gold leaf
flecks the curving walls, a flying lightness

levitates us toward the high-glazed
halls of disbelief & art,
of heaven.

Incarnation

I say you must hold my heart
between the roof and the floor:
between yawning gates,
hinged jaws of where it waits
like something on the way to gone—
half-swallowed, irretrievable, fuchsia-

sodden heart of the cactus fruit,
darker than fist of obsidian.
Your teeth rear up around it
like Stonehenge stones, like mah-jongg
tiles like terrible stiff
blonde pompadours hard
hard white chocolate rectangles.

You too yearning, toes hooked over
the edge, center so far forward the swoop's
inevitable: my cactus heart in your mouth
quivering, leaking out over everything
—purple lip, Yosemite chin, white shirtfront
residue of the immaculate life before.

The Rain

On, on, the drops fall and gather, until they're released from the tree.

I'm wakened to remember this, that to myself I am a questioning,
responding voice first in the hierarchy of feeling, more than any reflection
the eye could find on the surface of drops where they join and pool
at the base of an aspen.

There's no one else here to be received, to be gently bidden or begged
to be anything for, or with, me, to be my release from this voice
or to resemble rain or even to become the elemental instruction, incarnation
of joy. Instead, I attend to the sound unwavering of rain and under it,
the recollected music of thought, his, as he asked himself what is most
essential: love, or the other insistent gathering.

Wrong Sonnet: Mystery

If ghosts are real, they're professional strangers.
If real, I owe you an apology. You can laugh at me
in this and in our past lives—
in laughter we shudder together.
If knowledge from before this life is
in our cells what couldn't we know—
medicine we grow, gather without purchasing.
If knowledge from outside ourselves survives
then by what particle or current
will I encounter it from the ground,
my ears filled with birdcall, rushing
trains, my morning arms sore
blue and only a small cavity to hold
this strange, two-chambered faithfulness.

Third Eye

I say
part of the eye has seen loss
part waits for it—

yet two horses mild as mild
dogs came into the house—

You say
we could agree to love them
while you read a book of accidental humor

in an etching, cylindrical engines
blow the man overboard
back onto the ship
aloft on fonts of water frothing
comic as sea-monsters to science

you tell me, Science
the mouse in my stomach is doubt
     is the animal fear   wriggling

yet   sleeping naked I go closer to beloved
you naked in a distant state

as Buddha on the bathroom counter
holds something gold, maybe a lotus
or a flame, between planes
of his soles' Limoges

a grey horse settles down on kitchen floor
before we touch her—
gladness fills the room

sunning the waiting, cracking it
open, on the prow a shark's jaw
painted

open

O golden   O gold

Tom McDermott

KATHLEEN WINTER was born in McAllen, Texas. Her poems have appeared in *AGNI, The New Republic, Field, The Cincinnati Review* and other journals. Her awards include fellowships from Vermont Studio Center, Virginia G. Piper Center, and the Prague Summer Program. She is a graduate of the University of Texas, Austin; Boston College; the University of California, Davis, School of Law; and Arizona State University. Winter lives with her husband in Sonoma County, California, and teaches writing at the University of San Francisco.

TITLES FROM ELIXIR PRESS

POETRY

Circassian Girl by Michelle Mitchell-Foust

Imago Mundi by Michelle Mitchell-Foust

Distance From Birth by Tracy Philpot

Original White Animals by Tracy Philpot

Flow Blue by Sarah Kennedy

A Witch's Dictionary by Sarah Kennedy

The Gold Thread by Sarah Kennedy

Monster Zero by Jay Snodgrass

Drag by Duriel E. Harris

Running the Voodoo Down by Jim McGarrah

Assignation at Vanishing Point by Jane Satterfield

Her Familiars by Jane Satterfield

The Jewish Fake Book by Sima Rabinowitz

Recital by Samn Stockwell

Murder Ballads by Jake Adam York

Floating Girl (Angel of War) by Robert Randolph

Puritan Spectacle by Robert Strong

Keeping the Tigers Behind Us by Glenn J. Freeman

Bonneville by Jenny Mueller

Cities of Flesh and the Dead by Diann Blakely

The Halo Rule by Teresa Leo

Perpetual Care by Katie Cappello

The Raindrop's Gospel: The Trials of St. Jerome and St. Paula by Maurya Simon

Prelude to Air from Water by Sandy Florian

Let Me Open You A Swan by Deborah Bogen

Cargo by Kristin Kelly

Spit by Esther Lee

Rag & Bone by Kathrym Nuernberger

Kingdom of Throat-stuck Luck by George Kalamaras

Mormon Boy by S. Brady Tucker

Nostalgia for the Criminal Past by Kathleen Winter

FICTION

How Things Break by Kerala Goodkin

Nine Ten Again by Phil Condon

Memory Sickness by Phong Nguyen

LIMITED EDITION CHAPBOOKS

Juju by Judy Moffat

Grass by Sean Aden Lovelace

X-testaments by Karen Zealand

Rapture by Sarah Kennedy

Green Ink Wings by Sherre Myers

Orange Reminds You Of Listening by Kristin Abraham

In What I Have Done & What I Have Failed To Do by Joseph P. Wood

Hymn of Ash by George Looney

Bray by Paul Gibbons